WHALES
and
DOLPHINS

Troll Associates

WHALES
and
DOLPHINS

by Francene Sabin

Illustrated by Pamela Johnson

Troll Associates

Metric Equivalents

1 inch	=	2.54 centimeters
1 foot	=	30.5 centimeters
1 mile	=	1.6 kilometers
1 pound	=	.45 kilogram
1 ton	=	.91 metric ton

Library of Congress Cataloging in Publication Data

Sabin, Francene.
    Whales and dolphins.

    Summary: Describes the large sea mammals, related to
cattle, sheep, and deer, which are interesting for their
intelligence, their gentleness, and their adaptation to
the ocean environment.
    1. Whales—Juvenile literature. 2. Dolphins—Juvenile
literature. [1. Whales. 2. Dolphins. 3. Marine animals]
I. Johnson, Pamela, ill. II. Title.
QL737.C4S23   1985   599.5   84-2709
ISBN 0-8167-0286-1 (lib. bdg.)
ISBN 0-8167-0287-X (pbk.)

The sea is filled with many wonders, and each one seems more remarkable than the one before. The most wonderful of all may be the dolphins, which are also called porpoises, and the whales. From the four-foot-long harbor porpoise to the largest animal in the world—the blue whale—these intelligent creatures have been fascinating to humans since ancient times.

Although they live in water, whales and dolphins are not fish and are not related to fish. They are mammals, and their closest cousins are such land animals as cattle, sheep, and deer. And they are all probably descended from the same ancestor who lived long ago.

Scientists believe that about fifty million years ago some land animals began to look for food in the water. Then, little by little, they began to spend more of their time in the water.

After millions of years, they had become well adapted for living their entire lives in the water. Their bodies had become as streamlined as the fish around them. But they continued to be like their land-living cousins in many ways.

Like all other mammals, whales and dolphins have lungs for breathing air. That means they must rise to the surface to breathe.

But these sea animals do not have noses like their land-living cousins. Instead, they have an opening, called a blowhole, near the top of the head. Because of the blowhole's location, a whale or dolphin doesn't have to come very far out of the water to let out air and take it in. The blowhole opens for the brief time it takes for the whale or dolphin to breathe. Then, as soon as the animal dives underwater, the blowhole closes.

These sea mammals can dive very deep in their hunt for food and stay submerged for many minutes. The sperm whale, one of the largest of the sea mammals, can dive to a depth that is more than twice the height of the Empire State Building. In addition, the sperm whale can stay submerged for as long as an hour before it has to come up for air.

When whales and dolphins go to sleep, they do not sleep for very long. They usually nap underwater for five or ten minutes at a stretch, during which time they do not breathe. Then they wake up and go up for air. Scientists believe that the blowhole closes during sleep, so water will not pour in and drown the sleeping animal.

Like all mammals, whales and dolphins are warm blooded. This means their body temperature is always the same.

To keep warm in the cold ocean water, whales and dolphins have a layer of fat, called blubber, under the skin. This fatty layer is about an inch thick in dolphins and about a foot thick in the largest whales.

Because of their fatty protection, extreme cold doesn't bother whales and dolphins.

They generally stay away from the far reaches of the Arctic and Antarctic regions during the colder months, but not because of cold. The main reason is that there is danger of being trapped under the ice and not being able to come to the surface to breathe.

Adult whales and dolphins are not covered with hair the way most other mammals are. Grown-up whales have only a few hairs around their blowholes or on their chins.

The sea-going mammals give birth to living young and nurse them with milk, just as land mammals do. A baby dolphin is born tail-first. As soon as the baby is born, the mother helps it swim to the surface to take its first breath. The mother, also called the cow, is assisted by another female dolphin. The two adult dolphins swim with the calf, or young dolphin, between them. They protect the baby from the bumps of other playful dolphins and from the more serious dangers of the sea.

16

Whale and dolphin milk is high in fat and protein. It helps the calf grow quickly and build up the layer of fat it needs. When the calf of a blue whale is born, it weighs about two tons, or more than a fully grown elephant. And it is twice as long as most automobiles.

For its first few months the young blue whale gains about two hundred pounds a day. Fully grown, a blue whale weighs as much as eighteen elephants. And if it could stand on its tail, it would be as tall as a ten-story building.

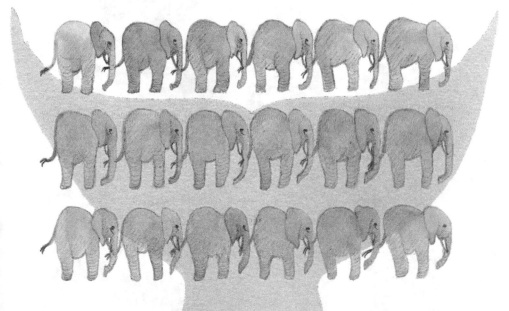

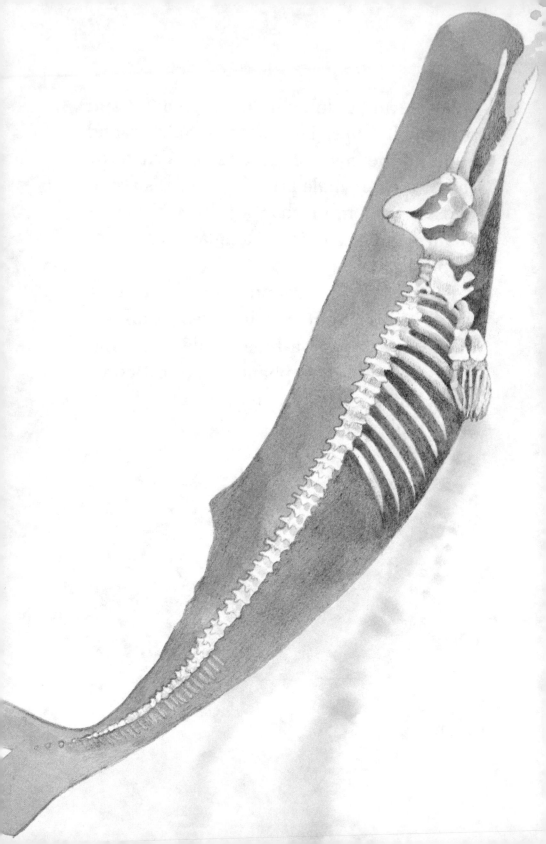

Whales and dolphins are vertebrates, which means they have backbones. But unlike land mammals, sea mammals do not have four limbs. They have just two front flippers, which they use for balancing, steering, and stopping. On the outside, the flippers look like the fins of a fish. But on the inside, there are bones similar to a hand with five fingers.

Whales and dolphins are powerful swimmers. They move swiftly through the water by beating their strong tails up and down. The tail is made of two fins, called flukes, which stick out sideways. This is different from a fish's tail, which has fins that point from top to bottom rather than from side to side. Scientists believe that whales and dolphins have sideways flukes because they are air-breathers. The position of the flukes helps them to swim quickly to the surface when they need to breathe.

Dolphins and toothed whales eat fish, squids, and octopuses. The large dolphin known as the killer whale also eats other sea mammals, such as walruses, seals, and even other whales and dolphins. They are called killer whales because they hunt other sea mammals, not because they attack people. Like other dolphins, they are very intelligent and friendly to humans.

Some whales are called baleen whales. Instead of teeth, these whales have strong, flexible plates of baleen growing down from their upper jaws. Baleen is a material just like your fingernails. It is also called whalebone, even though it isn't bone.

The baleen plates are very long and have fringed, bristly edges. As the whale swims, it takes in huge amounts of water filled with plankton. Plankton is the name given to the tiny plants and animals that live in the ocean. After the whale takes in the great amount of water, it closes its mouth, and then pushes its large tongue against the baleen plates. This forces the water back into the ocean. But the plankton is trapped by the plates of baleen, and the whale swallows it. In a way, the baleen is really just a giant strainer in the whale's mouth.

The baleen whales include the blue whale, the finback whale, the gray whale, and the right whale. The right whale got its name years ago, when whale oil was used for lighting lamps. The right whale was a slow swimmer and easy to catch. It also did not fight much. So whalers said it was "the right whale" to go after.

Baleen whales are different from toothed whales in another way. They have two blowholes instead of one. But the holes are so close together that it can be very hard to see that there are two. There are times, however, when a double spout of spray rises into the air above a whale. This is a sign that the whale that is breathing out air is a baleen whale.

The misty spray is the whale's warm, moist breath condensing as it hits cold air. This is just like the mist you can see when you breathe out on a winter day.

The blowholes of all whales and dolphins have another important use. They are used for communication. Whales and dolphins can squeal, whistle, chirp, mew, click, and make many other sounds. And all of these sounds come through the blowhole.

Although no one is certain exactly what the sounds mean, scientists know that the sea mammals are sending each other messages. These sounds may be signals of danger, a call that food is nearby, or a way to make sure no member of the group gets lost.

The sounds made by whales and dolphins also seem to be a kind of direction finder in the darkness of the water. Just as bats bounce sounds off objects as they fly in the dark, whales and dolphins bounce sounds off objects as they swim underwater. This

process is called *echolocation*. Sound travels much better underwater than it does in air, and with their supersensitive hearing, whales and dolphins can pick up sounds made many, many miles away.

In recent years, people have come to realize how very smart these sea mammals are, how gentle they are, and how well they are adapted to their environment. For all these reasons, scientists are increasing their studies of the mysterious world of the sea mammals. And who knows where this research will lead? One day, we may even be able to communicate with these fantastic and beautiful creatures of the deep.